My Dog's P.O.V.
(and How He Sees the World)

My Dog's P.O.V.
(and How He Sees the World)

Copyright © 2018 Still Water Literary, LLC

All rights reserved. No part of this publication may be reproduced or utilized in any form by any means, electronic or mechanical, including photocopying, recording, or by any information storage and retrieval system, without prior written permission from the publisher.

Library of Congress Cataloging-in-Publication Data

Upton, Howard, 1969 -
My Dog's P.O.V. and How He Sees the World

ISBN – 978-1-946811-04-2

1. Animals. 2. Pets. 3. Animal adoption 4. Relationships

Still Water Literary, LLC ™

Dedication

This book is dedicated to the many men and women who work tirelessly in animal shelters around the world, especially those working diligently to find good homes for animals without families. Most likely, you are underpaid and under-thanked, so this book is dedicated to you!

I would also like to dedicate this book to Cathy, my wife, who puts up with Rex, T-Bone, and me. I don't know how you do it, honey, but I'm glad you do.

Lastly, this book is dedicated to my mom, Peggy, and my step-father, Harvey. They each decided to host animals in their home as a part of their pet sitting service. They love and care for other's animals like no one I have ever seen. People who leave dogs and cats in their care know they are in the best hands in the world. How they deal with all those animals on a given day or night, I have no idea, but we are all happy they love those dogs and cats the way they do!

Acknowledgements

No written work is ever complete without acknowledging those directly, or indirectly, involved in its publication. Fiction and non-fiction writers alike share a common bond—a need for others to be involved in the creation of the work.

First, Abbie McGuire for spending time correcting my obvious grammar and spelling errors. Thank you for doing that for me.

I would be remiss if I didn't acknowledge Cathy, my wife. She encouraged me to pen this short work after I posted a blog with a few sentences I imagined between Rex and me. I went kicking and screaming because my passion is action/adventure writing, but in the end she was correct. This story needed to be told, not only because we dearly love our pets, but because she feared I was losing my mind with the talks Rex and I had (and continue to have).

Lastly, to you the ever faithful reader. You withstand my rambling blogs, overbearing social media posts, and tolerate my occasional video uploads. You are the best, and once again, I offer my undying gratitude to you all.

The Points of View

Preface
Chapter 1 **On Rolling in Crap after Getting a Bath**
Chapter 2 **On Always Wanting MY Food**
Chapter 3 **On Sleeping on the Couch**
Chapter 4 **On Driving**
Chapter 5 **On Chasing Birds and Rabbits**
Chapter 6 **On Prison Life**
Chapter 7 **On Being a Eunuch**
Chapter 8 **On Putting Our Shoes on the Furniture**
Chapter 9 **On Sleeping in our Bed**
Chapter 10 **On Sniffing Tires**
Chapter 11 **On Fishing from the Pier**
Chapter 12 **On Politics**
Chapter 13 **On Riding in the Boat**
Chapter 14 **On Watching Me Write**
Chapter 15 **On Seeing Snow for the First Time**
Chapter 16 **On Meeting T-Bone**
Chapter 17 **On Growling at Other Dogs**
Chapter 18 **On Eating T-Bone's Food**
Chapter 19 **On Grunting**
Chapter 20 **On Passing Gas**
Chapter 21 **On Luggage**
Chapter 22 **On Escaping Our House to go Explore the Neighborhood**
Chapter 23 **On Starring in a Commercial**
Chapter 24 **On What Comes Next**
Chapter 25 **On Staying with Me When I Am Sick, and Asking You to Adopt**

Preface

In October 2014, my wife and I drove through Anniston, Alabama on our way home to Augusta, Georgia. I received a call two days earlier from a friend who managed an animal shelter after he learned that Cathy and I might be in the market for a small house dog. My conditions to him were: non-aggressive, a non-yapper, and a dog with a lot of personality.

"You've got to see this dog, brother. He's a cool little joker," Kevin reported.

"Alright," I replied, "we'll stop by this Saturday and check him out."

After making the one hour drive to Anniston from our second home in Alabama, we walked into the front lobby of the shelter and waited while Kevin retrieved the dog. Cathy had remarked two or three times on the drive over that she was not certain she was ready for the responsibility of a dog, most especially one we did not know or raise. I explained to her that we could check the dog out, and if it was not a good fit simply tell Kevin "thank you, but this isn't the one."

We agreed that my approach was the right one, and I could tell that she was not very enthusiastic about a potential adoption, at least at the moment. As we waited, a door opened in front of us and out walked Kevin holding a bizarre little brown creature with the longest legs I have ever seen. Kevin was obviously a man with some experience and took the dog directly to Cathy who held and began stroking his short hair.

She looked at me and muttered, "Awww."

That was all it took for us to leave with a new dog housed securely in a transport carrier headed to east Georgia.

On the way home we discussed names for our new dog. I wanted to call him Turd because he looked like a little brown turd with long legs. It should go without saying that I did not get my way, and after some bickering back and forth, we settled on Rex.

Rex is a big dog's name. When you hear it, it elicits pictures of pit bulls, Dobermans, Rottweilers, and Great Danes. Our Rex was an Italian Greyhound, or miniature greyhound that weighed in at a whopping ten pounds. I loved the play on his name with the vision of a big dog, so we immediately began calling him by his new name.

Getting to know him over the next few weeks was a little challenging. On a few occasions, he pooped in the house or would lift his leg to pee on our dining room table. Breaking him was my job, so I would put his nose next to his mess, swat his little butt then throw him outside. This routine was beginning to grate on our nerves, as Rex just was not grasping the concept of peeing or dropping a deuce in the yard.

I was working on my second novel and would often find Rex lying by my feet as I wrote. He was strange in that he never barked; in fact, he lived with us for three days before we ever heard him do so. Cathy and I both thought something was wrong with him, that is, until I researched the breed and learned that they were not yappers. Other than dropping poop biscuits and watering our table, Kevin had done a pretty good job of locating him for us.

It was during one of those evenings as I was writing and Rex was lying by my chair that I noticed something peculiar. He sat up and began shaking as he stared straight at me. It was November, the house was warm, and there were no loud noises to scare him. I picked him up and held him close to me.

"What's wrong, buddy?" I asked.

"I need to pee," is exactly what I thought I heard in my head.

I put him down and walked into the kitchen and opened the door which lead to our back yard. Immediately, Rex ran outside, found the most interesting thing he could locate, and raised a leg to wet his surroundings.

Two things happened at that very moment—Rex began training Cathy and I for whatever it was he needed. We learned his body language and behaviors and responded in kind. Rex and I also began having conversations, to which I would imagine his response. His little face screamed experience and logic and our "talks" would play out in my head as though I was speaking with another human being.

Yes, I realize many of you are probably thinking that I should seek psychological help, and you are likely correct. All that said, Rex, Cathy, and I have grown very close and the conversations I have with him are downright entertaining. I have catalogued many of these discussions for you, my dear reader, to enjoy and read at your leisure.

Lastly, it my fondest wish that you consider adopting a dog or cat and save them from an untimely demise. So many little animals long for a good home, but are forced to spend a lifetime in a cage with minimal human interaction. I understand that raising a puppy can be joyful and loving, but I promise you, the bond between an animal freed from a cage and its adopted parents is insurmountable!

On Rolling in Crap after Getting a Bath

Invariably, I will give Rex a bath, dry him off then wait a little while before letting him go outside to do his business. On more than one occasion, he has seen fit to run around our relatively large spread in Alabama only to locate a pile of raccoon feces roughly the size of a large boulder. Without hesitation, Rex will throw himself into the pile and roll around in it, wet raccoon crap hanging from his short hair and smelling like a wastewater treatment plant in August.

Reading his mind when he runs out the back door is not difficult. He will stop for a few seconds, shake the remaining water from his coat then take off into the back yard in search of anything to make him smell worse. Rex is a one-dog accident waiting to happen.

Our conversation during and after his bath is as follows. Note: raccoon crap is the worst, most vile smelling stuff on the planet. If you have not experienced it, I recommend continuing to live a good life for the which the rest of us are envious.

"You aren't the easiest dog in the world to bathe, did you know that?" I asked Rex as I lathered him.

"I don't really like baths, so that makes perfect sense," he responded.

I shook my head and sighed, "Look, I give you a bath because I love you and want you to smell nice. Dirty dog smell is terrible."

"'Terrible' is such a judgmental word. You realize before the advent of bathing, dogs ran with their wolf kin and we all enjoyed each other's odor," he replied.

I shook my head again. It seemed as though each time I had a conversation with Rex, the tendency to shake my head grew.

"You have an answer for everything, don't you? Fortunately for us all, mankind came to the realization that soap and water alleviates poor hygiene. So, hold still while I finish washing you," I explained.

Rex's ears drooped backward on his head and his tail began wagging, "Can you rub my happy spot?"

"Talk to daddy like that again, and I will knock you out," I yelled!

"I was joking, Daddy. Sheesh, you have violent tendencies," he pleaded.

"I am not a violent person. Now, let me get you out of the tub and dry you off," I said as I picked him up and began toweling his wet hair.

"Oh yeah, I like that. Rub my back harder. Now my ears, dry behind my ears," Rex exclaimed!

"You are high maintenance, do you know that?" I asked.

Rex sat down and stared up at me, his tail wagging and tongue hanging out and to the side of his mouth. This was his typical response when he attempted to be cute. It worked. He is a cute dog.

A few minutes passed as Rex ran around the house. His short hair made the drying process much quicker than dogs with longer, shaggier manes. That was a benefit for all parties involved as he jumped and pounced on furniture in ritualistic fashion after getting a bath.

"Now that you're dry, do you need to go outside? I figured you needed to pee after taking a warm bath," I told him.

"Oh boy, Daddy, you are so right! I need to pee like a Russian race horse," Rex replied.

"Where did you learn that expression? Have you even seen a Russian race horse?" I asked.

Rex shook his head and said, "Can you work with me, please? The expression is merely a colloquialism frequently used by those of us in dire need of a bush or something upon which we would like to urinate."

Rather slack-jawed at his explanation, I opened the door and watched him run into the yard. Within seconds his head perked up as something grabbed his attention. His head moved in the obvious motion of one catching a whiff of something vaguely familiar. In a shot, he was running toward some overgrown weeds and bushes.

"Dude, you better not get dirty right after your bath!" I scolded.

"No worries, Daddy. I just want to check the smell out over here," he mused.

I watched as he jumped into the growth and promptly began rolling around. His tail was wagging frantically and his tongue flopped in utter doggy ecstasy. Rex rolled to his back and scratched on the ground like a grizzly bear against a tree in the forest. After a full minute of rolling around, Rex runs back to me covered in raccoon feces.

"WHAT IS WRONG WITH YOU? I just gave you a bath and the first thing you do is find a pile of crap to roll in? Do you have any idea how disgusting you smell right now? Do you have any idea how mad I am at you? WHY DO YOU ALWAYS FIND A PILE OF RACCOON CRAP AND ROLL AROUND IN IN IT?" I scream.

Rex lifted his head, his ears drooped, and his face solemn then said, "Daddy, it's really quite logical if you stop and think about it. I spend my life making friends and learning about other dogs by sniffing their butts. Rolling in a pile of dookie is no different than you splashing a little cologne on after you shave. Mommy likes it, doesn't she? And you see Molly next door? She digs my dookie smell, because now I smell like one big butt."

On Always Wanting MY Food

As always, Rex sat at my feet while Cathy and I ate dinner. We attempted to have a discussion, share idle chit-chat about our day, current events, and the weather, but neither of us could concentrate because we felt those eyes burning through the sides of our heads. He watched as we forked food into our mouths, the look on his face growing more pitiful by the second, even though his own bowl was filled with food and water.

"Can't I just eat my food without the 'poor, pitiful me' puppy dog eyes?" I sighed.

Cathy laughed and started to answer, "Well..."

"Not happening," Rex interrupted.

"I swear to all that is holy, you look like one of those starving dogs from a television commercial. I can almost hear it now—Just fifty cents a day can feed Rex for a whole year. He prefers baked chicken and McDonald's fries, but will eat almost anything you give him so long as it isn't high quality dog food," I replied as I shook my head.

Rex's tail fell between his legs as he managed to look even sadder than usual.

I sighed again and handed him some food. His ears perked up and gobbled it down without chewing. Rex acted as though he had never eaten human food.

"That was so yummy, Daddy! May I have some more?" he asked.

"No. Go away, and stop staring at me," I said, the exasperation in my voice more than evident.

On cue, Rex dropped his tail again resuming his role as the caged, starving animal begging for love and food. His eyes instantly became rheumy, and had I not known better, I would have sworn tears welled up on his bottom eyelids. This guy was a master manipulator and I was getting sick and tired of it!

"Man, I am really hating you right now," I told him as I handed him another bite.

"I love you so much, Daddy! May I have some more?" he asked.

"Two things, Rex—one, I applaud you for your good grammar. Not every dog is capable of proper diction. Two, right against the wall you have a dish full of your own food. I would very much enjoy eating my human food, watching the news, drinking my water, and conversing with my wife without the constant distraction of you staring at me. Is that too much to ask?" I finished.

His head dropped for a few seconds then popped back up, his head tilted to one side. "I understand, Daddy. I apologize for begging and disturbing you and Mommy during supper."

I reached down and patted his head, relieved he was starting to appreciate my perspective.

"May I have a drink of your water, Daddy?" Rex asked.

"What? If I was an animal abuser, you would be beaten right now. Go drink your own water," I exclaimed!

"But yours is cold and it's so hot outside, Daddy. My water is ambient. That means room temperature. I heard that on The Science Channel. Anyway, I realize room temperature water is better for digestion, but it doesn't have the aesthetic appeal that yours has in that fine piece of crystal," he pleaded.

I put my glass of water on the floor and watched him lap as much of it into his mouth as his tongue could reach. To say he has some level of control over me is an understatement. I draw the line with beer though. No matter how much Rex begs for a sip of my lager, he ain't getting it!

On Sleeping on the Couch

Rex, like many dogs, thinks our couch belongs to him. In his mind, it is like one giant daybed and serves as his own personal lounge area. If you attempt to sit beside him he glares, his discontent after being awakened from his three hour power nap obvious.

Recently, I opened the back door to let Rex take care of a nature call. Afterward, he ran back inside and hopped onto the couch. I sat next to him only to receive "the look." We stared at each other for an eternity until one of us finally blinked. As was usual, I engaged him in conversation.

"Rex, you cannot be more than fourteen inches long, but somehow you manage to take up an entire couch. Why can't you sleep in your own little doggy bed?" I asked.

"No can do, Daddy, and if you push me off the couch, I'm going to jump right back up here and crowd you out of my spot," Rex replied.

Despite his warning, I picked him up and sat him on the floor then laid down so I could watch a little television. He stood there looking at me with utter contempt. For a few seconds, he sat on his haunches as though he was pondering his next move. Unsurprisingly, he was and made a quick move to jump back onto the couch.

He landed around my feet before making his way along the space between me and the back of the couch. After inspecting the area for a few seconds, he nestled into a spot then worked his long legs and paws into my back as he attempted to push me off the couch.

I could feel my eyes narrow as I attempted to give him my own version of 'the look' "You don't wipe your paws when you come inside then proceed to track dirt all over the couch. That makes me irritable."

His eyes fell to his dirty paws then slowly rose until they met mine. A look of disdain fell upon his face as he slowly and meticulously began to lick his dirty doggy pads. When he finished, he smacked his lips and yawned.

"Is that better," he asked, his voice dripping with sarcasm and discontent?

"No, it's not better," I replied before continuing. "There's still the part about you taking up all the room on the couch. Why don't you let me lie down and sleep at my feet like a normal dog?"

He jumped to his paws and yelled, "Unbelievable! Humans go out of their way to capture my ancestors, domesticate us, and then have the audacity to complain when we lay on their precious furniture!"

"What are you saying? Are you calling me racist?" I asked.

"Don't be stupid. I'm a dog. I don't have a race," he replied.

"Fair enough. Will you get down so I can stretch out on the couch now?" I begged.

"No way, but I'll tell you what I will do just for you. See my tiny dog bed over there with just a small portion of padding beneath it? The one you and Mommy thought would match the furniture in the living room?" he asked.

"Yeah, I see it. What about it?" I responded.

"You can lay in it," Rex said.

On Driving

One of Rex's favorite things to do is riding in Cathy's car or my pickup truck. He especially enjoys the truck because he can see so much more since the truck sits higher than most vehicles. On occasion, he decides my driving skills are not sufficient and attempts to take over, usually while I'm neck deep in traffic.

For a few minutes, he will stare out the window. He will press his wet nose on the glass of the driver's side door leaving streaks in its wake. After those few moments pass, he will invariably turn his attention back to me.

On a recent trip, he and I enjoyed some interesting banter, which ultimately turned to him asking that question all kids request of their parents. I hoped it would not come to that, but invariably, he asked and I was forced to respond.

"Can I take the wheel, Daddy?" he asked as he hopped into my lap.

I ignored his question for a moment as we traveled westbound from Georgia to Alabama on Interstate Twenty. We had crossed over the Alabama state line minutes earlier and passed through the Talladega National Forest, an area thick with extremely tall yellow pines, oaks, and wild dogwoods. Our surroundings were beautiful and some that I always enjoy seeing while driving that section of highway. At last I glanced down at Rex and responded to his question.

"Buddy, I would love for you to drive, but I could get in a lot of trouble if I allowed you to slide into the driver's seat," I explained.

He thought for a few seconds as he stared out the window. I could see the gears turning in his tiny little head as he processed what I had told him. Eventually, he turned his attention back to me.

"Why would you get in trouble?" he inquired.

"Well, for one thing, you don't have a driver's license. And there's the obvious issue of your legs—they are too short to reach the pedals. Finally, I feel confident when I tell you that your ability to drive a standard transmission is non-existent," I told him.

He considered what I explained for a couple moments before turning his head to stare out the passenger side window again. I heard him take a deep breath before he responded.

"The world is a complicated place, Daddy."

"Yes, son, it is. The world can be cruel to even the best intentioned," I smiled at him.

He nodded his head in agreement before jumping back onto the passenger seat and looking out the window. His nose was pushed against the window and I smiled as its wetness added new streaks that I would later clean.

"I hope you aren't upset that you can't drive, buddy," I said to him.

"Nah," he replied. "I am more upset that we can't stop so I can pee on all those trees."

On Chasing Birds and Rabbits

As a miniature greyhound, Rex is built and runs like his full-sized brothers. To say he is fast is an understatement. His ten pound body is made up of eight pounds of leg weight, each of which are approximately sixteen inches long on his twenty inch tall frame. I have personally watched him cover three acres of ground in just a few seconds. If he was an NFL wide receiver, his forty yard dash time alone would net him a thirty million dollar contract.

Rex knows he is fast and loves to show his speed off to any and all wildlife. Whether it be birds, snakes, dogs, cats, rabbits, skunks, possums, or raccoons, Rex does not discriminate. The problem (or not, depending on your own point of view) is that he never bites or harms the other animal. He simply enjoys chasing it and showing his unearthly speed in a way the other poor thing has never before seen.

I once watched him chase a wild rabbit down, pounce atop it then stare at it until the rabbit struggled free. Rex watched as the rabbit hopped a goodly twenty yards before giving chase and, once again, jumping and landing astride the frightened animal. After another Rex versus rabbit stare-down, he unsaddled the hare and allowed it to jump into the woods adjacent to our house. Just as the rabbit's last paw was hidden from view, I would have sworn I heard Rex murmur, "That's right. You just got jumped by a house dog."

He really is quite arrogant about his racing ability, so one day I questioned him about his motives as he gave chase to a robin that was pecking away at the ground in search of a worm that would make a lovely afternoon meal.

"Why do you harass these animals, Rex? It's not like you are going to do anything with them if you catch them," I asked.

"This isn't about biting them, Daddy," he responded.

"No? Then why bother chasing them if you aren't going to do what most dogs do when they chase other animals?" I probed.

"Humans are such simple creatures, sir. There is a particular hierarchy in the animal kingdom. Perhaps you've heard of Darwin's theories of natural selection and evolution?" Rex proffered.

I sighed, "Of course I have heard of Darwin's Theory of Natural Selection. What does that have to do with anything?"

"Well," he began, "Darwin also theorized that all animals will naturally evolve over time. Generation after generation will slowly mutate into something not quite similar, but not wholly different than the original father that sired them. You, sir, have made sure that I will not evolve, so I must position myself in this lifetime as the alpha-male at all times in my domain," he finished as he stared at the empty spot where his 'manliness' once resided.

"We need to get something straight, Rex. I did not have you neutered. When we rescued you from the shelter, the damage was done, son. Now, your take on Darwin's evolutionary theory still doesn't explain why you chase rabbits and birds when you don't intend to bring them harm," I replied.

"As I said, I must exert my dominion over those within my realm, although I cannot and will not, ever reproduce. Besides, do you think those birds and other animals have any idea that I won't bite them?" Rex asked.

"I doubt they have an idea that you will not harm them," I answered.

"Now you are beginning to understand my power, Daddy! I subject these unsuspecting critters to my speed and power and they run or fly back to their nests to spread the word about the Powerful Rexy," he said in a rather excited tone.

"You are on such a power trip. You need medical attention," I exclaimed!

"What I need is to catch another rabbit or finally catch a bird," Rex replied.

On Prison Life

Rex passionately refers to his time in the animal shelter as "prison." Any time I attempt to correct him by pointing out that he lived in an animal kennel where he received a steady diet of nutritious food and clean water, he is quick to point out that he was, indeed, in prison. His description of his time there makes it difficult to argue with him when he extrapolates how difficult it was to remain behind bars, and the solemn tone in his voice makes him sound very matter-of-fact about the whole ordeal.

To give you some background on Rex's imprisonment, it must be understood that both he and his sister* were dropped off at the same shelter on the same day. His previous owner described Rex as vicious, ill-tempered, and one to pounce on other dogs in an attempt to kill or maim them. Having gotten to know this docile animal over the years, and having watched him interact with numerous animals, it is blatantly obvious that his previous keepers either did not have the time to love him, the money to feed him and his sister, or simply grew tired of the responsibility that comes with having dogs in the home.

As I tell anyone interested in hearing Rex's story when his first family put him up for adoption, "This dog couldn't bust a grape if you put the grape in his mouth then closed it with a vice." He does tend to be a little territorial in his surroundings, but at no time has he ever hurt another person or animal. In other words, he growls a good game, but could not fight his way out of a wet paper bag.

The two of us sat on my recliner watching television. Specifically, we were enjoying one of my favorite programs: *COPs*. I watched as his head perked up when the cameras followed one man from the scene of the crime, through his arrest, and finally to a jail cell. That is when Rex began talking.

"Daddy, you can't imagine how terrible prison life was. I was in a cage, man. Water and a little food each day, paper to pee on, and daily PT for an hour was my routine. The prison guards were pretty nice, but some of the bigger dogs in cages next to me used to tell me they couldn't wait to sink their teeth into me and shake the life from my eleven pound carcass," he described.

"That sounds horrible," I replied.

"Yeah, and it got worse when I corrected them and told them I only weighed ten pounds. They thought I was just being smart-mouthed, but the reality is I didn't want other people to think I was putting on weight," Rex went on.

"Were you honestly concerned with how much the other dogs thought you weighed?" I asked.

"Daddy, a dog has to protect his reputation when he's in the big house," he told me. "Besides, I spent my time in the cage working out by doing pushups and sit-ups."

I sat there with a sly smile on my face, hoping he would not notice it. Rex was insanely sensitive about his time in the shelter and I did not want him to think I was discounting how scared he was to be there. Still, his description of it all reminded me of a Turkish prison, which almost caused me to laugh out loud. I controlled myself as he continued.

"Dude, there ain't no prison in North Korea that could touch what I went through. I was a D.O.W," he proclaimed.

"A D.O.W.?" I asked.

"A dog of war, Daddy. A. Dog. Of. War," he finished.

*My wife and I were distraught to find out Rex had a sister that was dropped off at the same time. Fortunately, she was adopted, although we would have loved to have them both in our home.

On Being a Eunuch

On numerous occasions Rex has accosted me regarding his being neutered. Each and every time we have this discussion, I remind him that the damage was done before we adopted him, but apparently when it comes to the subject of his testicles, all humans look and behave similarly. I cannot imagine the ribbing he took from the other male dogs while he was locked up at the shelter, but it was most certainly humiliating.

One day, while we were in the back yard, Rex stopped running long enough to sit down and scratch behind his ear. As he peddled away at the side of his head, I was busy working on a project started a few weeks earlier that I wanted to complete. I looked back at him for a second only to realize he had stopped scratching himself, but continued to sit with his leg in the air. Rex stared at his nether region for a few seconds before lifting it to look directly in my eyes.

"I can't believe you did this to me, Daddy," he said as his eyes lingered over the area where his testicles used to reside.

The look on his tiny little face spoke volumes. Most dogs have an innate ability to look sad, but Rex takes it to a whole new level. He has the ability to soften the hardest heart when his ears droop and his head hangs from his narrow shoulders. That is exactly the look he was giving me.

"Son, like I have told you a dozen times, I had nothing to do with you being neutered. In fact, I wouldn't have done it to you because I would have loved getting a puppy from you," I sincerely replied.

He continued to stare at the area where his manhood once resided then raise his head to look at me while shaking his head. At one point, I thought I heard him snivel and choke back a few tears. I felt sorry for him, but there was nothing I could do.

He stretched his neck before standing up, looked me dead in the eyes and told me, "All this and no female will understand what Rex-love is about. It's a shame, really."

I stared at him in disbelief. The words that sometimes rolled off his tongue were enough to leave me speechless and unable to respond. After a few years of our conversations, I am sometimes shocked by what he says.

A warm summer breeze blew through our trees as I continued to look at him. He refused to flinch, so we sat there staring at one another. A fly circled over his head, and I could tell he wanted to snap at it, but would not give in to the impulse.

"You should close your mouth, Daddy. This fly circling my head is going to fly right in if you don't," he said.

So is the nature of our discussions.

On Putting Our Shoes on the Furniture

Rex has a strange habit, when Cathy and I are not at home, of grabbing any of our shoes he can locate and putting them on top of our furniture. There have been times when it has taken us a full day to locate a pair of shoes because he is apt to place one on a couch and hide another under the covers of our bed. He will literally nudge his way under the sheets and blankets to hide one of our shoes.

On one occasion, I discovered a pair of Cathy's high heels in the family room. For those not familiar with the layout of our home, it is a split-level house with all the bedrooms upstairs, and the family, dining, and living rooms on the lower floor. Due to the incredible number of shoes she owns, one walk-in closet is dedicated to them and the vast quantity of clothes she has acquired over the years. This particular time, Cathy forgot to close the closet door and Rex promptly shot over the threshold, most likely before our car was backed out of the driveway.

When we returned, I saw Rex sitting in front of the couch, his face sad and worried. I knew immediately he was up to no good, so my eyes darted around the family room in search of whatever it was he was guilty of doing. On the couch sat the heels. I grabbed them and made my way upstairs to put them back in the closet. Doing this would prevent a serious scolding from his Mommy and save me from her wrath as well.

As I walked up the stairs, I inspected the shoes only to discover tiny little teeth imprints in one of the heels. Rex was following closely behind, as he always does when I go upstairs. I stopped to look at him and he dipped his head again in a telling shame. My silent stare spoke volumes: *When your Mommy finds this, you are dead. Do not scream for me either! I can't do anything to protect you, son.*

After this event, and a few others, we've learned to hide our shoes should we be forced to leave him alone for a couple of hours, or at least assure they are all in a closet with the door tightly shut. Initially, we believed his desire to move and hide our shoes was due to his dislike about us leaving him alone. He was, after all, our son and who leaves their son alone in a house without the ability to change the channel on the television? Rex and I sat down one evening and discussed his behavior and he explained it to me like this:

"I do not understand your shoe fetish, son. Why do you seek them out and put them on the couch or bed?" I questioned.

"Look, Daddy, I can only lick my butt for so many hours when the two of you aren't here. You leave your shoes within reach and all that runs through my mind is 'challenge accepted,'" he explained.

"I appreciate your candor, Rex, but a little couth would go a long way with me," I reprimanded.

I turned to walk away and heard him clear his throat as though he was trying to get my attention. Under normal circumstances I would ignore him because some of the stuff that comes out of his mouth leaves me dumbfounded. After hearing him out, I realized I should have heeded my own advice.

"What is it, buddy?" I asked, the hesitation obvious in my voice and posture.

"I have no idea what 'couth' is, Daddy, but if it tastes like your shoes I would love to have it," he exclaimed!

On Sleeping in Our Bed

When Rex first moved in to our home, we made him sleep in his own bed. He whined at first, most likely because he bonded strongly with us, and because he was now spoiled rotten. We showered him with love and he returned it in kind, but Cathy and I were adamant about him not sleeping in our bed. In fact, at first, we insisted that he sleep in his own bed in our living room, but he would sit outside our door and whine until we let him in. I did not realize at the time how he was training and bending us to his will. For a ten pound dog with a tiny head, he was most manipulative!

Cathy was away on business for a week, and I was left to work locally and care for the new addition to the house. I would leave on my lunch hour to drive home and check on him, let him to do his business, and play with him before leaving again. I felt bad about leaving him alone for four or five hours, but figured he was pretty resilient and had my shoes to occupy his time (see the previous story for details).

By the second night of Cathy's trip, Rex and I had grown even closer. Since Mommy was not in the house, he got my undivided attention and we would play until we were both pretty tired. I opened the door and let him outside for one more evening constitution before climbing onto our bed. Rex followed me into the room and sat down in his bed and stared at me with his big, sad eyes. I am not kidding you at all when I tell you this pooch has a way of looking at you that will make you believe he is homeless, starving, and in need of fifty cents in order to make it through the day!

I rolled over, my back to him, in hopes that he would lie down and go to sleep. The back of my head felt as though two small holes were being bored into it; I knew he was still sitting there giving me his most hopeless and desperate look. Sure enough, after a couple of minutes, I rolled over to see Rex sitting there, his head down, his ears drooped, and his rheumy eyes looking longingly into mine. My sigh was probably louder than it should have been what with his "I-was-recently-beaten-and-need-a-good-home" look.

"One night," I told him. "You can sleep with me for one night, but you better not tell your mom."

"It's a deal, Daddy," he cried!

Rex's long legs propelled him into our bed with ease. He licked my face before curling up against me and falling asleep. I chuckled quietly while I stroked the short hair on his back. Within minutes the dog was snoring!

The next night was a repeat of the previous one, only this time, much to my chagrin, Rex elected to take advantage of the charity I had shown him and jump into the bed without my consent. I put him on the floor and told him to get into his bed. The same downtrodden look and droopy ears once again appeared.

"Dude, you know you have your own bed. Why can't you just sleep in it?" I asked.

"Yes, Daddy, I know I have my own bed, but yours is so much more comfortable," he explained.

"I can see that, but the fact-of-the-matter is this isn't your bed," I told him.

Rex jumped onto the bed and licked my face again then asked, "Could you please turn the television on?"

"Why?" I asked, my exasperation apparent.

"I like watching the news before I doze off. It's my personal recipe for a good night's sleep," he replied.

I could not process what I was hearing. Rex telling me that he liked to listen to the news before he drifted off to sleep was as foreign to my ears as him seeing another country, yet there we were, having this talk. I took a deep breath and sighed audibly before reaching for the remote control and flipped the television to the news.

On Sniffing Tires

This issue is not a Rex thing, it is a dog thing, but I expect more from an Upton, even an adopted one. He cannot spend time outside without running to our vehicles to sniff the tires. I would not find the behavior strange if I happened upon what looked like urine from another animal and Rex was merely attempting to get its scent to catalogue for future reference, but he sniffs every tire on every car, including the wheel wells. This is, to me at least, peculiar.

"Normal dogs sniff the ground as they search for the perfect place to pee or poop. What is wrong with you?" I asked as he sniffed the tires on my truck.

Rex continued sniffing, but spoke to me as he did so. I was reminded of an archeologist so engrossed in his work that he could not pull himself from his duties for one second to converse. "I can't explain it. Some people with OCD have to have things placed in a particular order. I have to smell every tire on every vehicle within a two mile radius."

I tilted my head a trifle before responding, "Yeah, but sometimes you pee on them then sniff them again the next time you come outside. That's just a little gross if you ask me."

"I didn't ask you. Mind your own business," Rex replied.

"A good dog would not waste his time sniffing tires and such. Instead, he would sniff out lost treasure and money," I explained, probably just a little too hopeful.

"Sorry, Daddy. I am not enamored with those materialistic things, nor do I believe you should be. A love for the materialistic is unhealthy and unbecoming," he mused.

He continued around my pickup truck, pausing every few seconds to inhale deeply. Sometimes, I would hear him blow the air out of his nose quickly before resuming his inspection. If I did not intervene the sniffing would go on indefinitely.

"Rex," I began, the exasperation in my voice evident, "please just find a nice spot to pee. This should not take that long."

"One cannot simply wash away tens of thousands of years of canine evolution because one wants to go back inside the house," Rex explained.

"Fine," I said. "You stay out here. I'm going back in the house and getting something to eat."

At the sound of 'eat,' Rex sprinted to our door and yelled at me, "What's taking you so long, Daddy? Hurry up!"

On Fishing from the Pier

Cathy and I had a pier built on the lake behind our house. We figured since it was to be our forever home, we would make it as people friendly as possible; most especially since one of my favorite pastimes is fishing. After the pier was built, I purchased a very sturdy wrought-iron bench, which I placed at the end so I could sit in the early morning sun or evening breeze and wrangle a few fish onto my line. Quite often Rex would accompany me on these outings and sit by my side and watch me cast into the water, at least until he got bored.

On one such excursion, in the late afternoon hours, we were chatting about how nice the day had been despite the heat. The evening was hot, even in the waning daylight. Gnats and mosquitos buzzed our heads, but maintained a safe distance, due, in large part, to the vast quantity of deet I smeared all over my body.

Our conversation shifted easily from football to food. Eventually, we got on the topic of fishing, a subject I later felt bad for starting. Rex was quick to point out how rude I was for bringing it up.

"It would be pretty cool if you could fish with me. You know, like grabbing a fishing rod, baiting your own hook, and casting it into the water," I said.

Rex sat silently, his little eyes glaring at me with all the malice he could muster.

"What?" I asked, obviously confused.

"You're pretty cold-hearted, Daddy," he replied.

"What do you mean? I was just saying I would like for you to fish with me," I explained.

As he turned to walk away from me, he told me with some contempt in his voice, "I don't have any thumbs. You know I can't fish."

"I'm sorry, son and didn't mean any disrespect. What I was trying to say was it would be nice for us to share this experience together," I tried to explain, although I realized I was digging myself a deeper hole.

As he continued to trot back toward the house, I was sure I heard a "harrumph," escape his little mouth.

On Politics

One of my favorite topics is politics. Most people I know cringe at the very thought of engaging in something so diabolical and detestable. In fact, politics ranks right up there with talking religion and family problems in the world of "do not discuss" around people you know and love.

One evening while Cathy was away at the store and Rex and I sat on my recliner watching the news, I thought I would give the topic a go with him. Unsure of his political slant, I elected to ease into the topic, rather than dive headlong into specifics with him. My decision may have been a poor one.

"Hey buddy, do you have a particular political party with which you affiliate?" I asked Rex.

He lifted his head off my knee and yawned.

"I'm partial to the Dogatarian Party," he said.

"The Dogatarian Party, huh? What is the party platform?" I pondered.

"We don't believe in boundaries or fences, and are all-in for free range pooping and peeing. We believe in liberty for all canines, Daddy!" Rex stated.

"Well, that sounds a little chaotic, son. In fact, it sounds lawless with a dash of anarchy splashed on top for good measure," I goaded him.

His ears perked up at my description of his political party. He took a moment to stretch then stood upon my leg, his short nails digging into my thigh. I heard him take a deep breath in preparation for his response.

"Sure, Daddy. Our party is much different than the elite, rich humans running around spending other elite, rich humans' money while making promises they don't intend to keep, forcing unpopular legislation down their constituent's throats, and living in a white mansion with a private plane that takes them everywhere at other humans' expense," he mapped out for me.

I rubbed my chin and considered what my ten pound miniature greyhound just told me. At no time in our relationship did I consider that he would have such an astute take on politics as a whole, much less align himself with a doggy party the likes of which I had never heard. To my knowledge he had never lied to me, so there was no reason to believe he was now.

He continued, "Consider this—our country was established on a few basic principles, with few federal laws. States essentially self-governed and paid a pittance for a national army to protect the Nation's borders. Today, the federal government has taken on a grandiose position of power, which forces states to abandon their once cherished sovereignty. Along with usurping local power and independence, the federal government has established itself as an authoritarian lexicon, holding an individual citizen's money earned in a state as ransom should a state not comply with federal demands."

My jaw was slack and my face reddened. I could not believe what just flowed from his mouth to my own ears. Rex had mapped out everything I felt was wrong in the United States in just a couple of sentences. I did not know what to say or how to reply, so I did what any self-respecting human does when they are perplexed: I changed the subject.

"Don't you need to go outside and poop or something?" I asked him.

"Yeah, I am feeling a little bound up," he replied.

On Riding in the Boat

By now I am sure you have a good feel for the relationship Rex and I have developed. Unlike a lot of traditional "outside" dogs, he tends to be a prima donna and prefers the safety of our house and modern conveniences like central heating and air, as well as a Mommy or Daddy hand feeding him; he is truly spoiled. That notwithstanding, I attempt to offer Rex new and exciting adventures; experiences that he will take with him to the grave. In much the same manner that I raised my children, learning and seeing things first-hand are most often the best educational tools.

One of the many things I most enjoy is fishing. Specifically, fishing gives me much needed time away from the rat-race. More specifically still, sitting on the water is serene, relaxing, and stress free. Most specifically yet, fishing allows me time away from people, conversation, the Internet, driving, traffic, stores, and the general craziness that surrounds us all.

When I fish, I ask my little doggy if he wants to join me. In typical Rex fashion, he is excited about the prospect of traveling somewhere, but asking him to sit still and be quiet for an extended period of time is like asking a toddler not to pick things up and put it in his mouth. His attention span is the size of a thimble, and his ability to get distracted at the sound of a falling branch is second to none.

On such a day, I asked Rex if he wanted to go catch fish. He jumped around, his tail wagging, and his ears standing straight up. I took that as a resounding "yes."

I hooked the boat up to my old F-150 pickup and drove up the road to the boat launch. After backing the trailer into the water and releasing the boat from its metal and wood confines, I tied it off then parked my truck. I grabbed Rex and placed him inside the little v-bottom rig, untied her, and pushed off. Almost immediately, Rex grew nervous. He was not fond of being surrounded by water and confined to the small fishing boat. After running back and forth bow to stern, he finally settled down next to my feet and stared at me while I dropped the trolling motor and maneuvered us around the narrow lake in search of the perfect fishing spot.

"Are we there yet?" he asked.
"Please don't do that,"
"Do what?" he asked again.
"Act like a little kid anxious to get out of a car."
"Well, I want to get out," he exclaimed!
"Feel free to jump in the water," my curt reply came.
"That's really funny, Daddy. You know I don't like the water," he explained.
"Well, most dogs like to swim," I told him.
"I'm not most dogs," he replied.
"You are not wrong about that," I said, the sarcasm dripping from the corners of my mouth.

We moved along the water's surface at a slow pace, the little trolling motor spinning its propeller at top speed, which was not fast at all. I picked out a shaded spot inside a watery cove and dropped the anchor. After baiting my hook, I cast into the water and watched the bobber settle gently. Within seconds it was snapped under water. I jerked my rod to set the hook and reeled until the small bream was in the boat with us. A broad smile swept across my face.

"Look at that, son. My first fish of the day," I said to Rex.
"That's nice. Can we leave now?" he asked.
"If you don't stop whining, I'm going to toss you in the lake," my voice even.
"I will tell Mommy," he dared.
"You said you wanted to go fishing, so I took you fishing. Before we left, I told you fishing is something two

people do together in silence. We are here to be one with nature, and to do so in quiet contemplation," I attempted to explain one more time.

"When you are quietly contemplating," he began, "do you consider how much pain the fish will be in when you pierce its tiny little jaws?" he pondered.

"My God, Rex. Give it a rest. Please," I begged.

"I want to go home. It's hot out," he replied.

"Tell you what, how about I call Mommy, tell her to meet us at the pier, and I'll drop you off there?" I bargained.

"No, Daddy. I want you to come with me," he told me, his tail wagging.

"There is a distinct possibility I am going to take you back to the kennel and leave you there," I threatened.

"Daddy, don't ever say that," he shivered in spite of the heat.

On Watching Me Write

My sparse office is home to a few things. I have my desk, which holds upon its hutch my dry erase board filled with notes, plans for future books, religious statues acquired when Cathy and I travel abroad, some old DVD's, and a note pad. Also inside is a nightstand, but no bed, and a futon upon which Rex resides while I am working on a book.

Since we are connected at the hip, I do not mind him being here, but the futon sits directly behind my chair. I can feel him staring at the back of my head when I do not pay attention to him, which is a little unnerving, especially when I know he is upset with me (like the time we brought his new brother home—the topic of another chapter).

"I wish you would at least lie down on the floor beside me," I told him.

"Why?" he asked.

"I have a difficult time with anyone sitting behind me. I can feel you glaring at my back," I explained.

"Sounds like you have a guilty conscious," Rex quipped.

"That is not true. I like to think of it as a *survival instinct*. You know, like a caveman who had to sit with his back to the wall so he could watch the entrance to the cave in order to keep a predator from entering and eating him?" I replied.

"Daddy, I am ten pounds. I doubt I will be eating you any time soon," he said.

"You are missing my point," I told him.

"No," he said, "what you have explained to me is that you have some unfounded fear that has resulted in you feeling uncomfortable anytime someone happens to sit or stand behind you. Psychiatrists call this agoraphobia, or the fear of being unable to escape," Rex fired back.

My eyes blinked uncontrollably for several seconds, and my lips moved without thought. No words formed on them, as my brain raced to explain how Rex could possibly know a psychological term such as "agoraphobia."

Before I could ask, he rolled his eyes and said, "Dude…Google. Duh!"

"Wait, you're telling me you looked up my phobia on the Internet?" I was perplexed.

"I am not merely a warm and loving companion, Daddy. I have a brain too. It hurts to know you are just now realizing this," he said as his eyes narrowed.

On Seeing Snow for the First Time

Shortly after we adopted Rex, Cathy and I decided it was time for us to make the trek northward to Chicago so we could spend Christmas with her mother. It was expectedly cold up there; for it was late December and the wind was ripping and roaring off Lake Michigan. Fresh snow had fallen the night before we arrived, piling on top of the previous accumulation.

Rex's disproportionately long legs, as compared with the rest of his body, measure somewhere in the range of ten or eleven inches. He is capable of running like a normal sized greyhound and jumping like an NBA basketball player!

After arriving at her mother's house, we unloaded the car and said our "hello's." Corra, Cathy's mother, had visitors when we got there and everyone fawned over Rex and his cute face. Realizing he had not done his business for a few hours, I put my coat on, grabbed his leash, and led him outside for some much needed relief.

I stepped over the front door threshold but felt resistance in the leash. Rex stared at the blanket of white, the confusion obvious. I gently tugged on the lead, but the more I pulled the more he resisted.

"Man, come on. It's freaking cold out here. You need to pee, poop, or whatever so we can get back in the house," I exclaimed!

"What is this stuff, Daddy?" he asked.

"It's called snow, son. Now, let's go because I'm freezing," I told him.

With much trepidation, Rex placed one paw on the front porch. When it sank an inch or so into the white fluff, he pulled back again.

"There is no way I am going out there, Daddy. I'll pee and poop in the house," he said.

"You most certainly will not do that in the house. I am pretty sure if you do, a mystery meat breakfast will probably be served in the morning," I replied.

"There is zero need for violence," Rex reasoned. "That said, I am not stepping paw into the white stuff!"

I bent down and grabbed him then walked to the front of the yard, dog in one hand, poop bag in the other. The snow did not look deep, so I put him down so he could get busy. Another gust of wind hit me in the face and I turned away to avoid its worst bite. When I looked down at Rex, all I could see was the top of his head and the tip of his tail.

"You are a real comedian, Daddy! Now get me out of this," he yelped.

As quickly as I heard him scream he jumped like a kangaroo on hot Australian sand. Rex landed firmly in my arms without my having to bend to catch him! His little body shivered as he pressed himself close to my coat.

"I am sorry, buddy. I didn't realize the snow was that deep. Let's walk down the sidewalk and see if we can find an area without much snow," I reasoned.

Rex continued to moan and argue with me until I found a place in someone's yard without snow. It looked as though the homeowner had shoveled snow away for his own pet. I placed Rex onto the frozen grass where he sniffed for the appropriate spot to make a poo-poo deposit.

In true Rex form, he assumed the position and did his business. After he finished, I picked it up to carry it to the trashcan when I felt him stop and begin tugging the leash again.

"If I am going to freeze to death, I will at least pee," he said while staring at me.

"Okay, get busy so we can get inside," I urged.

He lifted a back leg and looked on in amazement as the white snow quickly turned yellow.

His eyes narrowed as he said to me, "Had I known my pee-pee would do that, I would not have protested as much."

On Meeting T-Bone

For a couple years, Cathy and I discussed rescuing another small dog so Rex would have a companion. At times I would protest the addition, telling Cathy that Rex was like an only child and bonded with us immediately. Bringing another animal into the house could be problematic.

Even though she worked from home, she could not break away from her computer to entertain and play with Rex. As a result, she felt sorry for the little guy. Eventually, I would relent.

My mom and step-dad dog sit in their homes. Several people from around my small home town bring their dogs (and sometimes their cats) for them to keep while the owners are traveling on business or pleasure. At any given time my mom's house would look like a fancy animal shelter when I visited.

One such family traveled often. Sometimes they would be gone for a couple months, as both traveled internationally. Their little dog, T-Bone was a shih-tzu mix with the cutest face in the world. After several trips, T-Bone's mother could no longer keep him and asked my mom if she knew of anyone willing to adopt. Naturally, she reached out to Cathy and me first.

We debated on whether to bring him into our home, as we sometimes travel and would have to dump both dogs on my mom while we were out of town. But after meeting him we decided we would take him to his new home and introduce him to his new brother. This is where things went awry.

From the very start Rex was not a fan. He growled at T-Bone, even though he would never bite him in a million years. He pounced on him with his long legs and raced to eat T-Bone's food after we would pour it into his bowl. Rex was acting like a spoiled little tool.

"Boy, leave T-Bone alone before I whoop your little butt," I warned.

"Take him back, Daddy," Rex demanded!

"I will not take him back and you will stop being mean to him. We brought him home so you would have a play buddy," I told him.

"You're my play buddy, Daddy. We don't need him," he argued.

"Listen, son, I'm not always here because I have to go to work each day. Your mom can't entertain you because she has a lot of work to do too. We figured he would be a great addition to our family because you sometimes look lonely," I replied.

"Oh, that," he began. "That isn't my lonely face. That is my *pet me now face*."

"Whatever," I sighed. "Just stop being mean to him. He is a good boy."

Rex nodded with his head to T-Bone who was laying on the couch. "He's a lump, Daddy. Look at him. He is nothing more than a hairy rug."

"We'll take him to the groomer," I countered.

"Great. Then he will be a groomed rug," Rex said, the exasperation in his voice.

"Why am I even bargaining with you?" I asked out loud, mostly to myself.

"Why? Because I'm your boy. Your numero uno amigo. I am the yin to your yang, the innie to your outtie. I am Robin and you are Batman! I am…"

"Stop!" I demanded. "I still love you but we are not getting rid of T-Bone. Remember your time in jail? That is where he was headed if we didn't take him in, so suck it up and deal with it. This isn't up for debate."

"I'm going to bite him when you aren't looking," Rex said as he trotted away.

"I will bite you back if you do," I threatened!

As he walked down the hall I heard him exclaim, "This is unfreaking believable!"

On Growling at Other Dogs

As I explained earlier, Rex loves to look out of the windows in both our house and our car when we are on a road trip. Watching him do so makes me wonder how much of the outside world he takes in and what he thinks of it all. Little nose prints are prevalent on the glass and we are in constant cleaning mode whenever the blinds are raised.

No matter where we are, if he sees another dog, he is quick to start growling and barking. While I appreciate his natural born instincts to protect his family and his dwelling, I must admit to rolling my eyes when he does it. More often than not, he becomes fixated on much larger animals before letting loose with a chorus of barks.

If I find time to write during the daylight hours, I do so from my office on the second level of our house. I will open the blinds and periodically gaze onto our neighborhood in search of the right word or phrase, or perhaps a subplot for current work. While I type away, Rex enjoys perching himself on the back of the futon so he can keep watch.

One of our neighbors has a large Labrador Retriever that she walks periodically. Any time Rex sees the animal he breaks into a barrage of ten-pound barks, growls, and pants. The hackles on his back stand up as he gives it his best effort to sound ferocious.

"Will you please stop that nonsense?" I yell.

"I cannot deny my innate urge to protect, Daddy. Of all people, I figured you would understand this," he stated.

"I did not say I could not understand it, Rex. What I did say was 'please stop.' I am trying to work, we are in our own home with the doors locked in the middle of the day, the lady across the street has that large dog on a leash in their own yard, and you are acting like an Asian Temple

Guard Dog. Besides being very annoying, I must admit the thought of your tiny jaws attempting to defend us against that large lab is laughable," I finished.

I regretted saying it as soon as it came out of my mouth. The look on tiny Rex's face was one of utter devastation and sorrow. It was as though he was a tiny little balloon that had been struck by a giant needle. In my mind's eye I could see him popping, his hopes and dreams exploding along with him.

"I'm sorry, man. I shouldn't have put it that way. I did not mean to say that you were incapable of protecting us in your own special way," my attempt at reconciliation a poor one.

His head sank lower and the blades in his back rose, making them more pronounced and his expression even more grievous.

"I said I was sorry. Let it go, Rex," I pleaded.

"Sorry doesn't fix anything. As an author I would expect you to know that words matter," the longing for sympathy evident in his voice.

"I'm a fiction novelist. I write to entertain, my friend. I leave academic writing to the academics," I reasoned.

"Oh, so it's my fault I feel like crap after you deflated my ego and kicked me in my imaginary testicles, huh?" Rex asked.

"Please don't tell me I'm dealing with a bi-polar or depressed dog. In all honesty, I don't think I could handle with that right now," I told him.

"How did you think I would react when you said that Sasquatch across the street would chew me up? Can't you see that I merely want to protect my loved ones?" He said.

I scratched my head and suppressed a smile as I listened to his pleas for pity. There was little doubt what he really wanted and needed after I upset him.

"How would you like a treat?" I asked as I rose from my chair.

Rex perked up. "Are you attempting to buy my love, Daddy?"

"Well, I suppose I am," I shrugged.

"Okay, I reckon I'm good with that. My love is yours for one chewy treat," he replied.

"Done," I said as we walked downstairs together.

On Eating T-Bone's Food

Rex is smart. We know it, he knows it, and anyone he has encountered understands the pooch has a degree of intellect. His primal need to be dominant, to sustain his place in the house as the alpha-male along with his brain power makes him devious at best, and a turd at worst.

When we adopted T-Bone, his previous owners gave us his wire cage, his bed, his food, and his dishes. I point this out because T-Bone's food and water dishes are distinctly different from Rex's. T-Bone's dishes are white and separate, as in they are two different bowls. Rex's dish, on the other hand, is a single purple, two-compartment thing. Standard Wal-Mart pet food holding fare.

Cathy went to great lengths to separate their dishes when it was time to feed them; one on one side of the kitchen and the other on the opposite side. No matter the placement, Rex deemed it necessary to push T-Bone out of the way and dive-bomb into his food. The food we fed them, as it were, was the same. This made little difference to our jealous trouble-making Italian Greyhound who figured this roost was his to rule.

"Rex, get out of T-Bone's food," Cathy yelled! "Hon, get your dog out of here while poor little T-Bone eats."

"Get over here with me, Rex," I demanded.

"That is not happening until you get rid of this cretin, Daddy," he replied.

"I'm not asking you, Rex, I'm telling you to leave his food alone," I said, my voice growing ever sterner.

Rex stopped eating T-Bone's food long enough to look up at me and smack his lips. Afterward, he dropped his head into T-Bone's dish and continued indulging. His tiny stomach began to bloat, distended by the gross quantity of food he was consuming. I looked into Rex's dish and saw that it was gone, Rex having eaten all of it before moving on to T-Bone's dish.

"That's it, you are out of the house for a while," I stated.

I grabbed Rex and picked him up, carried him to the back door, and deposited him onto our patio. The yard is fenced in, so he would have dominion over it while I let T-Bone eat his food.

"Daddy, you can't do this to me. That little bastard is the devil," he screamed as I closed the door!

I leaned against the wall and took a deep breath before looking down at T-Bone.

"Alright, buddy, Rex is outside, so you can eat in peace," I told him.

"Thanks, Pops, but I'm really not hungry. I was anxious to see you toss Rex out of the house though. Thanks again for making my day," he spat.

I stood there, my mouth agape as I pondered what I just heard.

"Wonderful," I said to no one in particular, "another smartass."

On Grunting

Rex grunts more than any dog I have seen or heard in my life. Touch him while he is asleep and you will get a resounding, "uhhhhhhhh" in return. Move him while he sits on your lap, "uhhhhhhh." Pick him up while he stands on his rear paws to greet you, "uhhhhhhh."

It is as though I am an occupier in his world, and touching him without permission is an invasion of his space and time. He reminds me so much of my own children that it is rather spooky.

"What in the world, man? Why are you grunting?" I asked Rex as we sat in my recliner. He was perched on my leg while I watched television.

"You touched me," he replied.

"So? I don't grunt when I'm touched," I offered.

"I am trying to sleep and you are putting your hand on my back. That is grunt-worthy," Rex said.

"My lightly touching you while you nap for the nineteenth hour today is grunt-worthy, huh?" I enquired, the sarcasm, as usual, dripping from my question.

"Daddy, a dog like me requires beauty rest. God built this thing of perfection that you are petting. I figure the least I can do is protect his investment," he said as he dropped his head onto my lap once again.

On Passing Gas

Rex loves to lay in our laps while we watch television. Sometimes, he will nestle himself between my leg and the arm of my recliner then bury his nose into the crevice formed by my leg and the seat cushion. At first, I thought this a cute and cozy way for him to position himself. That is, until the first time he broke wind and almost made me throw up on my own lap.

To say that Rex can smell up a room is an understatement. He has at his disposal the ability to make an entire room gag in a fraction of a second. Before we go any further, I realize this is not the most pleasant topic; you should be Cathy or me when this ten pound dog crop dusts us like a single engine plane on a mission to control insects on a 1,000 acre farm!

I must admit a particular pleasure watching Cathy's reaction when Rex is on her lap and lets loose of a nasty one. She has an acute sense of smell, which happens to amaze me, and anything just a little obscenely scented will make her gag or throw up. I doubt she appreciates the hilarity, but rest assured it always gives me a great belly laugh!

"Rex," *gag, cough, cough* "did you just fart?" Cathy belched.

"Why yes, Mommy, I did. Is there a problem?" Rex asked.

"Oh my God, I'm going to be sick," she gagged.

Rex and I both watched as she hopped up from her seat and bolted to the bathroom. She closed the door, but it was not enough to hide the sounds of her retching. I knew better than to laugh out loud because Cathy would get mad at me, so I covered my mouth in an effort to suppress and sound that might escape it.

Rex sat on her chair as she gagged and I chuckled. His expression was blank, perhaps even a little confused. I could tell he wanted to ask a question, but I suppressed the urge to ask him what he wanted to say. There was little doubt that he would not hold back, but I could find no reason to encourage him.

"What's wrong with Mommy?" he asked.

"Buddy, you farted on her," I replied.

"So? I do that all the time," Rex said.

"I know, but your farts are disgusting," I proclaimed!

"They most certainly are not, and I can prove it," he stated.

From behind the door Cathy retched for what seemed like the tenth time. At long last, we heard the toilet flush followed by the sound of running water from the bathroom sink. I turned my attention back to Rex.

"You can prove your farts aren't disgusting?" I asked, the doubt made obvious in my question.

"Yes, I can," he nodded.

"Well, stop wasting time and tell me before you Mommy gets out here and starts yelling at you," I demanded.

"Every time I make a bad smell, you laugh, Daddy," he said matter-of-factly.

"That's it? That is your measuring stick?" I laughed. "You do understand that I laugh when I fart and your Mommy smells it, right?"

"You're right, I don't understand," he replied as another look of confusion lit upon his little face.

"This is a game that Daddy's play with Mommy's all over the world. Most of the time, Mommy's do not appreciate the game, but that doesn't stop Daddy's from playing," I explained.

"I want to play," Rex said, his tail wagging back and forth.

"No son, you do not get to play that game. In fact, I suspect in a few seconds, after your Mommy opens that bathroom door, that you will come to fully comprehend what it is that I have been trying to explain to you," I told him.

The sound of the bathroom door fell upon us, and if ever a look of fear could befall a dog's face, it did so at that very instant. Rex hopped onto my lap and buried his head in one leg. His tiny eyes watched as his Mommy walked into the family room and her gaze bore into him like something spawned from Hell itself.

Before she could get a word out of her mouth, Rex darted off my chair and ran upstairs where he hid out the remainder of the evening. She turned her furious eyes on me, but I cut her off before she could begin.

"I don't like that dog. He is disgusting and rants on like no child I've ever heard.

"But," I continued, "you must admit his sense of understanding when his Mommy is upset is pretty keen," I smiled.

Her lower lip trembled and I could tell she was struggling for what to say, so I got up and gave her a hug.

"You know you still love him," I laughed.

On Luggage

As I have noted and you have come to realize, Rex is smart and wiley. He senses much, sees all, and processes more than we will ever know or understand. He has also grown to appreciate luggage and what it means.

Whenever Cathy or I pull down baggage and begin packing, Rex knows he is about to travel, although he likely does not understand his final destination. More often than not, he and T-Bone will be traveling to my mother's house for a stay while Cathy and I are out of town.

That aside, he will whine and whimper because he believes we are going to leave him behind; that is, until we open the front door and tell him to get into the car. When he hears "car," his little tail starts wagging five hundred miles per hour. In case you are wondering, T-Bone is so laid back he doesn't care one way or the other. He is game for whatever we plan on doing or not doing. Low Maintenance T-Bone is the polar opposite of the Rexinator.

"Daddy! Daddy! Daaaaaddeeeeeeeee!" I heard him scream across the family room.

"Son, stop yelling. You're giving me a headache," I tell him.

"Okay, sorry, Daddy," he politely replies as he eyeballs the bag I am picking up.

"Daddy! Daddy! Daaaaaaddeeeeeeeee!" He yelled again.

I felt a sudden pain in one side of my neck as my head snapped in his direction. His beady brown eyes were locked on mine in some strange canine anticipation. For a brief second, I wanted to grab him and yank his tongue out of his mouth, but those beady eyes turned my cold heart warm again.

"What did I just say to you," I asked?

"I know, Daddy, I know," he paused before continuing. "Am I going with you?"

"Yes, you are going with Mommy and me. Now will you calm down so I can finish loading the car," I asked?

"Okay, Daddy," he forced from his lungs as he jumped up and down on the couch.

"Daddy! Daddy! Daaaaaaddeeeeeeeeee!" he screamed a third time.

I imagined dropping the bag from my hand as though it were an appendage belonging to someone else, I watched in silent awe as my fingers reached for his tiny throat.

"You are making my head feel as though it will split in two with all your yelling. This is your last chance to quiet down," I hiss.

"Okay, Daddy. There is really no need for you to exhibit this violent side you have demonstrated here today. For future reference, you may want to consider anger management, as I have read that this type of behavior could lead to hypertension, which left unchecked could lead to stroke or heart attack," he finished.

"Where have you heard such a thing," I asked, my ire suddenly tapering off at his response.

"Television, of course," he looked at me, nonplussed.

"You heard that on television and remembered it," I pressed?

"Yes. What else is a young man to do while his Daddy is away at work all day," he posed?

I paused to scratch my head. Rex had taken me off guard, and, even though I understood the game he was playing, I was amazed at his level of intellect and craftiness. My reply to him was just as smart and creative. I furrowed my brow, picked up my bag, and nodded at him as I turned and walked to the garage.

"Daddy! Daddy! Daaaaaaaaddeeeeeeeeeee!" I closed the garage door and paused long enough to catch my breath and convince myself I did not want to beat him.

On Escaping Our House to go Explore the Neighborhood

Rex is not really the type to run away, per se. As an Italian Greyhound he is, however, one of the most curious dogs I have seen or met. Like any person on vacation, he loves to explore new places, sniff new tires, and urinate on other people's shrubs or lawn decorations. I see no abnormality in his behavior. By the way, an escape from the norm is a vacation to Rex!

All this aside, Rex is a house dog and does not understand the concept of traffic or what would happen should a car treat him like a speed bump. On the few occasions he has escaped our house (either by fleeing through an open door, or squeezing through an opening in our fence), Cathy and I have given chase to both get him back in one piece, and to talk him into understanding that there is "no place like home."

We also have a secret "go to" when or if he leaves, which I shall share in a moment.*

His first escape involved shooting out the front door of our house and sniffing every shrub on our street. Naturally, he also urinated on most of them, stopping long enough to sniff our neighbor's front doors. He trotted from home to home in search of God knows what, while I followed along behind trying to grab him.

"Rex, get over here!" I exclaimed.

"Nope, not going to do it, Daddy. I have a lot of territory to cover, other doggies to meet, and tires to sniff. You go home and I will be along shortly," he replied.

I shook my head and kept up the chase as he continued his onslaught through the various yards while he sniffed and peed. For a few seconds I was certain I saw a smile on his little face.

When he stopped to check out a neighbor's door I figured my chance at catching him would never be better, so I lunged and threw a leg in front of his passageway to the next yard.

With no effort, Rex sprang over my ankle and ran to the next yard. He laughed as he ran, looking back long enough to stick his tongue out at me.

"Hahahahahaha! Did you really think I would fall for that trick, Daddy?" he asked.

I watched him sprint to the next house then the next, pausing long enough to admire the tires on several cars, or to pee on flowers and shrubs. The cycle was vicious and I was out of breath. It is usually at this point when I begin threatening him.

"When I catch you, I'm going to beat your butt!" I yelled.

He turned to face me with a quizzical look on his face. "Was that meant as a way to get me to run to you? Really, Daddy, do you think I want to come to you now that you have proclaimed how you will beat me upon falling into your arms?"

The more he tried to sound like a canine Shakespeare the more I wanted to yank his teeth from his mouth. I was exasperated, tired, winded, and angry. For a brief second, I considered taking him back to the shelter and dropping him off as a form of punishment. As that thought came and went, I watched as he stopped to stare at a potted plant on another neighbor's doorstep.

The look of innocence and shear wonder made me smile even though I was still upset with his behavior. At long last, I squatted down to catch my breath. Rex turned and looked at me again. He dropped his ears and wagged his tail then took off at top speed and sprang into my arms.

"I love you, Daddy! I knew you would eventually want to play with me!" he screamed.

I realized that by squatting, Rex believed I was stooping to his stature so we could have a little father-son time. In that instant I rolled to my back and we played for a few moments while he wagged his tail and licked my face.

The front door to the house opened and a neighbor I had never met stepped onto her front porch. The look on her face said it all: Why are you two idiots playing in my front yard?

As quickly as I could, I grabbed Rex and tried to explain to the lady what had happened. She simply rolled her eyes, opened her front door and stepped back inside without so much as a "goodbye." And just like that, a magical moment was forever lost.

*As I wrote earlier, Rex loves to ride in the car. We learned through a couple of escapes that if we hit the key fob and he hears the chirp, he will come running! That is when we grab him and carry him into the house. He falls for it every single time.

On Starring in a Commercial*

Traveling and meeting people has been a blessing to me. Whether for work or pleasure, when I am flying around the United States or outside my country's borders, I make a concerted effort to meet new people and engage in meaningful conversation. Not only does this make time go by a little faster when I am sitting in an airport or in a restaurant by myself, real person-to-person talk is much more mentally stimulating and profound than simply texting or typing a message on a social media platform.

In the workplace, we refer to meeting new work peers or higher ups as "networking." I suppose the same could be said about my interactions with people I have met while traveling. If I find the person particularly interesting, or vice versa, we will exchange contact information and try to remain in touch. Some examples of people I have met while traveling that I consider interesting:

- A major league baseball umpire
- A senior vice president of a firm that develops engines used to support rockets and rocket boosters
- A professional explorer and marketing genius
- A tour guide in Bangkok, Thailand.
- A St. Louis news anchor
- A porn star actress (the conversation was very interesting)
- An oil tycoon en route to Hong Kong for business
- A professional American football player born and raised in Cameroon, Africa
- An infomercial star
- The owners of a huge hearing aid franchise

- A restroom attendant at a famous restaurant in Las Vegas
- A young lady in the midst of starting up her own clothing line
- A bartender at the Dallas/Ft. Worth Airport (who I got to be friends with over time)
- A marijuana farmer disowned by his family in Virginia after relocating to Colorado to start his business

These are all people I have met throughout the years that I have maintained some level of contact with—yes, the restroom attendant is one of the most hilarious. I suppose you would have to have an elevated sense of humor to do his job, but he does it with pride! All that aside, I have also maintained a friendship with someone I have known for many years.

This young lady works for a marketing firm that, at the time, was in charge of a commercial shot in order to promote a new brand of dog food. She sent out a survey to many pet owners she knew asking if we would like to participate. I discussed the possibility with Rex about him becoming a video star of some sort, to which he replied, "Meh, I just want to try some new food."

He is my kind of guy.

Within a couple of weeks after replying about our interest, the final selection was made and twenty-five dogs of all sizes and breeds descended upon Nashville, Tennessee in a rain storm for the commercial shoot. I was excited. Rex was happy we stopped at McDonald's along the way. He was even happier when I bought him some fries.

"Daddy, can I have another one?" he asked.

"Son, you know you always have to poop after eating. Why don't we stop before you lose it in the car?" I replied.

"Not this time, Daddy. Just one more?" he begged.

I handed him a single fry that he grabbed from my hand and gobbled down. In an attempt to keep him from being parched, I wiped as much of the salt from the fries as I could. We were an hour from Nashville, so I figured he would be okay.

About ten or fifteen miles from our destination, Rex got a case of the "poop shakes." This is what he does when nature calls. He doesn't whine or whimper, or even claw at the door to let you know he needs a potty break. He simply sits and stares at you as he shakes like a leaf on a tree.

"I told you not to eat that last fry," I chastised.

"It most likely wasn't the last one I ate that piled inside my tummy, Daddy," Rex quipped.

"Well, just hang in there a few more minutes and we will be there," I told him.

"I'll do what I can, but if the little browns start knocking on my back door, I will probably have to let them out," he replied.

"You have some serious, serious issues," I told him.

He managed to wag his tail after my remark, which let me know he was laughing on the inside. I hoped and prayed that his inside laughter would not cause an explosion in the car. Fortunately, Rex did not have an accident and I was not forced to power wash the inside of my car before leaving Nashville.

I pulled into the parking lot of the studio and quickly fastened Rex's leash to his collar. He pounced across my lap as soon as I opened my door and began pulling me toward a bush then onto a patch of grass. Once he finished his business, we walked through the double glass door and stepped inside the lobby. Already present were about ten dogs of various sizes. Rex bristled without looking at me.

"Stay behind me, Daddy. I can take these dogs," he warned.

"Listen, James Bond, I don't need you to protect me. These dogs and people are here for the same reason we are," I explained.

"Who's James Bond?" Rex asked as he eyed the other dogs.

"Never mind, just relax. Go sniff a butt or something," I told him.

"Good idea, Daddy," he said.

Rex stretched the leash as far as it would go as he followed my directions. Dog after dog got his or her butt sniffed then followed up by returning the favor. After a few moments, most of them had become lifelong friends.

Other dogs and their owners continued shuffling in as the skies opened and rain began to fall. Everyone wiped their feet and paws, signed the registration form, and took a seat.

Frolicking and sniffing continued for another fifteen minutes, after which we were all told to assemble and follow my friend inside the studio. We were greeted by a brightly lit white wall, a camera sitting atop a large boom, and employees scurrying around with shoulder mounted cameras or sound equipment.

Rex looked up at me and began, "Daddy, what in the he…"

"Man, how many times do I have to tell you to watch your language? Now be cool until we get some directions," I ordered.

Like a teenager, he responded, "Okaaaaaay. Sheesh. There is no reason to get all bossy."

I cut my eyes at him and gave him *the look*. The look always worked on my daughters, but does not phase Rex in the slightest. I suspect the reason it is not as effective is because his attention span is that of a half-ounce of water streaming through a large sieve.

We were directed to sit or stand around the props set up in the studio so we "looked natural." Rex's eyes zipped around the room taking in everything there was to see. He zeroed in on someone standing close to us.

"Hey Daddy, check out that blonde," he whispered.

"The lady right there?" I pointed with my chin.

"No. I could care less about another human, Daddy. Look at that cute little Bichon. She's a doll," he proclaimed.

As I am wont to do when Rex speaks, I rolled my eyes and tried to ignore him. He continued to tug on the end of his leash in an attempt to get closer to the little dog he had spied. The Bichon finally noticed him and pranced toward us like she was the belle of the ball. They took turns sniffing each other's butts; I was certain this love affair would last at least the remainder of the day.

The camera panned around the group as we stood or sat as nonchalantly as possible. We all wondered what we were supposed to do and were instructed to just act naturally. In true Rex fashion, he looked directly at the camera then looked to the right.

"What are you doing?" I asked.

"I saw the camera on the boom staring at me, and gave it my left side. My profile is so much more appealing," he explained.

"I don't know how much more of this sh.."

"Daddy! Language around the ladies," he said.

"Sorry," I replied, my response not very sincere.

After a short time passed, my friend Wenonah (the marketing guru) told each of us the order by which we would be interviewed. I had not expected a solo appearance, so I brushed off my finest jeans, clicked the heels of my cowboy boots and picked my tiny dog up because we were second in line.

It occurred to me at that moment that several other men were in the room, most with large manly looking dogs. Then there was me…and Rex, the smart-assed Italian Greyhound without an Italian accent. I considered the irony for a moment, given that I am a pretty big guy.

"You know, if you spoke with an Italian accent, your cool factor would go up several levels," I said to Rex.

"You know, if you would stop holding me like you were a New York City debutant your cool factor would increase by tenfold," came Rex's snide remark.

"I honestly cannot stand you," I said as I looked him in the eyes.

He started to say something, but thankfully we were called to the interviewer's area where a director's chair stood. I placed Rex on the chair and turned to face the camera and the man asking questions.

"Move over. The camera should be focused on me, not you," Rex chided.

"Shut up," I hissed.

"What?" the interviewer asked.

Realizing he could only hear one half of the conversation, I blushed and shook my head as if to say, "Nothing, let's move on."

He asked several questions about Rex, his eating habits, activity level, and personality. I stopped him because I was laughing.

"What's funny?" the man with the microphone asked.

"Rex is a smart ass and has the personality of a serial killer," I explained.

"What...the...what?" he stammered.

"Okay, let's just edit that out," I said.

The interviewer's face was one of confusion, but in keeping with the time-honored profession of asking questions to someone facing a camera, his face once again became stoic. Rex looked up at me while I spoke to the man with the mic. From the corner of my eye, I could see his little face. There was no doubt in my mind that he was on the verge of saying something to embarrass me. And then a second round of the doggie shakes began.

"Daddy, you've got to speed this up, because I need to drop a deuce," he said under his breath.

I felt a smile creep across my face; the interviewer was none the wiser. In a few moments, we wrapped up the interview, I grabbed Rex and we headed for the door. He turned to look at me as we walked through lobby.

"Grab a poop bag, Daddy. This is going to be a good one!" He told me.

Note: At the time of publication, the commercial was not yet complete. Also, the commercial was not intended for distribution on television, but retail merchandisers attempting to market the new pet food.

On What Comes Next

Ninety-nine percent of the time, Rex is hyper-active and ready to play. His ability to leap from one piece of furniture to the next is unprecedented and without comparison. Those long legs of his propel him through the air like a ten year old on a trampoline, usually landing him right on my groin.

At other times, he is eager for Cathy or I to open the door allowing him free reign in the yard. It is hard to believe that a ten or eleven pound dog can trounce so loudly that he sounds like a grown horse on the open prairie. As he sniffs, runs, stops to pee then runs some more, he will regularly stop to make sure we are watching him. His desire for attention is non-stop.

There are other times, those fleeting moments, when the world seems to come to a halt for him and he takes a moment to consider, as Douglas Adams famously penned, life, the universe, and everything. It is in those moments that I realize Rex's tiny brain is full of wonder, and the inquisitive look he retains on his face always makes me smile.

As I sat outside in our back yard listening to the cicadas buzz and the frogs croak in the waning hours of a summer day, Rex was his usual jovial self. He bounded along the fence line in search of God knows what, but search for it he did. His nose upended leaf after leaf, and limb after limb, as he sought out an animal or insect he felt like intimidating. After a half-hour of fruitless searching, he ran to me and hopped in my lap as I sat on our patio bench.

Rex curled up and lay down while I stroked his back, I watched as he closed his eyes and began drifting off to sleep. A few minutes passed before I saw him open his eyes a blink. His brow furrowed and I could tell something was on his mind. Under normal circumstances, I cringe when I realize Rex is about to ask or say something, because what comes out of his mouth is generally unpredictable. This time, however, was different and I could tell he was in a serious state of mind.

Rex slowly lifted his head and stared up at the darkening sky. I watched as his dark brown eyes darted across the horizon taking in the last vestige and daylight and the onset of nightfall. A few sparkling stars appeared sporadically in the purple haze of evening, and he looked at them as though it was the first time he had taken notice of their existence.

"Daddy, what's up there?" he asked.

"Well, there are stars, other planets, other moons, and a whole lot of nothing in between," I replied.

My response seemed to confuse him more.

"You mean there are other people and animals out there?" he wondered.

"I don't know, son. Maybe there are. If so, we haven't discovered them yet, and they haven't discovered us," I explained.

He seemed to ponder on my words for a few minutes before continuing. In the seconds that followed my explanation, I watched as he gathered his thoughts. The little gears in his mind were churning and working overtime.

"So, where do we go when we die, Daddy?" he continued.

"Son, what has got you in such a serious mood?" I asked.

"Well, I have seen birds and other animals that die, and I was wondering where they go, or do they just go into the ground and that's it?" Rex mused.

"That is a question that has been asked since man and animals first began walking the earth, Rexy. I believe we have an immortal soul and it goes to Heaven after we die.

When we get there, we are reunited with all of our loved ones who have died before us," I told him.

"What is a soul, Daddy?" Rex asked me.

"A soul, as I understand it, son, is that magical essence that gives living, breathing creatures their lives and personalities. It is the very thing that makes us unique. Some have referred to our souls as the 'breath of God'," I told him.

"Wow! Do you think I have a soul, Daddy?" he asked, his innocent eyes looking directly into mine.

"I sure do, Rexy, I sure do. In fact, I am certain you have a soul, son," I told him.

"How can you be so sure, Daddy? Maybe God only wants people to be in Heaven?" he continued, his voice sad and serious.

"I will tell you how I know you have a soul, son. I know this because God wants us to be happy all the time when we get to Heaven. No hurt, no pain, no missing anyone. I would be very sad without you with me, so I know you have a soul and after we die, we will be together in Heaven," I finished.

"You make me happy too, Daddy. You know what? When I die, I will still be happy because I know God will let me watch over you," he replied matter-of-factly.

I paused for a few seconds and brushed a tear away from my eye.

"That would make me feel very happy, son," I said.

"Are you crying, Daddy?" he asked.

"Shut up," I said as I gave him a tight hug.

On Staying with Me When I Am Sick, and Asking You to Adopt

Rarely do I ever get sick, but like most men, when I come down with something it seems the world is at its end. Rightly so, Cathy does not want to be around me for fear of catching my man-cold, but the constant I do have is Rex. Without fault, when I do not feel well, he is by my side.

While I lie in bed Rex will jump atop the mattress and gingerly walk toward my face for a closer inspection. I try to push him away because I worry about him getting sick too, but he simply walks back to me with a look of sympathy and worry.

After finishing his inspection, Rex will curl up next to me so we are back-to-back. Without a doubt, he knows I am not feeling well and is doing what he can to keep me warm and safe.

There is rarely any conversation of substance when he does this; his intuition never ceases to amaze me. Usually, I stroke his back with my hand and tell him I love him. He will lift his head and reply, "I love you too, Daddy. Get better so we can play."

The love and affection he shows me often feels undeserved on my part. After all, we just wanted a small house dog to share our home with, but Rex took the adoption to a whole new level. He realized how lucky he was to escape the animal shelter no matter how well they treated him.

What I think he fails to understand is how much he means to our family. He makes us laugh when we do not feel like laughing, and he makes us happy when it feels like we could not be happy. Rex has been a Godsend for Cathy and me. In these final words I would ask you, the reader, to consider adopting an animal, rather than purchasing one from a breeder.

To be honest, I never considered pet adoption. In fact, Cathy and I really didn't want a pet at all. We were married for several years before the topic was broached, and to this day I cannot explain why we elected to get a dog. Hindsight being what it is, we are both happy it ended the way it did.

I do not want anyone to believe I am against dog breeders and someone making money. On the contrary, I am a self-described capitalist pig who enjoys every part of business and do not condone stifling a person's ability to make money. But there are thousands of animals without loving homes, and tens of thousands of them that wander our streets that will likely starve to death or be killed by a passing vehicle. Other animals will be taken to shelters where they will be euthanized.

These animals were brought into the world on purpose or accidentally. In both cases, it behooves us a species to take care of them if we can. With both Rex and T-Bone, I believe they understand that we love them and want them to be happy. Each animal has a glorious way of demonstrating to Cathy and me what we mean to them and nothing makes us happier.

So, please consider visiting a local animal shelter if you are in the market for a new companion. Give these animals a second chance at a happy life before you run out and spend money on a dog or cat. I doubt you will be disappointed by your decision, and cannot imagine that the animal you bring home will be upset when he or she no longer has to spend a lifetime in a cage or kennel.

Check out Howard Upton's other titles available on Amazon.com, Barnesandnoble.com or his personal website howardupton.com

Of Blood and Stone: A Bill Evers Novel
Occam's Razor: A Bill Evers Novel

If your local bookstore does not carry Howard's books, please request they do so!

About the author:

Howard Upton is the author of the highly acclaimed Bill Evers action/adventure novels. He has also had articles in distinguished martial arts magazines published over the years.

Howard is a husband to Cathy who works tirelessly in an effort to keep him in line and focused on what is important. He is also a father to four beautiful daughters and a son, all of whom he refers to as his wonderful group of financial burdens.

When he isn't busy being a husband or father, Howard teaches karate and judo to a select group of students that he hopes will continue to spread the arts he loves and enjoys.

Howard also thrives on traveling the globe with Cathy, meeting new and exciting people, while seeing and doing things he could not otherwise do in the United States. His most recent trip to Thailand will likely resurface as a scene in one of his upcoming novels, as he quickly grew enamored with the country while visiting it.

He and Cathy split time between homes in Alabama and Georgia and work hard on maintaining a loving marriage while cooped up in the same car traveling between the two.

Howard can be contacted through his personal website: www.howardupton.com

About Rex:

Rex is a long legged, hyper-active Italian Greyhound with a profound interest in all things pertaining to life, philosophy, and dog food. He grunts if he is touched while sleeping, and has an uncanny ability to clear a room with his silent flatulence.

He splits time between homes in Alabama and Georgia, while gazing endlessly out of car windows during the trek between the two. His cold, wet nose manages to smudge each car window from which he stares, leaving constant reminders for everyone that "Rex was here."

He can be reached through his daddy's website, www.howardupton.com and is available for speaking engagements.

Contact Howard Upton through his website:

www.howardupton.com

www.ingramcontent.com/pod-product-compliance
Lightning Source LLC
Chambersburg PA
CBHW071410040426
42444CB00009B/2186